THE TIMELY ADVENTURES of CAPTAIN CLOCK

D1355263

Franklin Watts
First published in Great Britain in 2018
by The Watts Publishing Group

1 3 5 7 9 10 8 6 4 2

Credits
Art: Pol Cunyat
Design Manager: Peter Scoulding
Cover Designer: Cathryn Gilbert
Production Manager: Robert Dale
Series Consultant: Paul Register
Executive Editor: Adrian Cole

HB ISBN 978 1 4451 5714 6
PB ISBN 978 1 4451 5715 3
Library ebook ISBN 978 1 4451 5716 0

Printed in China

MIX
Paper from
responsible sources
FSC® C104740

Franklin Watts
An imprint of
Hachette Children's Group
Part of The Watts Publishing Group
Carmelite House
50 Victoria Embankment
London EC4Y 0DZ

An Hachette UK Company
www.hachette.co.uk

www.franklinwatts.co.uk

THE TIMELY ADVENTURES of
CAPTAIN CLOCK

TONY LEE AND POL CUNYAT

LONDON·SYDNEY

DON'T FOLLOW US, TIME COPS! OR THE SMALL CHILD GETS IT.

HEY! LEAVE MY SISTER ALONE!

JESSIE!

MILLIE!

FWAM!

THEY'RE GONE. BUT DON'T WORRY.

WE'LL GET YOUR SISTER BACK.

TO THE CHRONOGRAPH! WE DON'T HAVE A MINUTE TO LOSE!

IT'S A TIME TRAVELLING SHIP. WE CAN LOSE ALL THE MINUTES WE WANT!

FASHION

ROME — 44 BCE.

THE SWORD OF MARS HAS BEEN STOLEN!

CAESAR! WAS IT VIKINGS?

BEARDED MEN? YES! THEY TOOK THE SWORD --

-- THEN DISAPPEARED LIKE MAGIC.

BLAST! WE MISSED THEM!

CAESAR. BILL SHAKESPEARE, BIG FAN. I'M WRITING A PLAY BASED ON YOU.

TELL ME, HOW DID YOU FEEL WHEN BRUTUS MURDERED YOU?

BRUTUS? MY BESTIE? HE WOULD NEVER KILL ME!

GUARDS! GET THEM!

SORRY!

11

ALL SIX PIECES OF ARMOUR CAN TRAVEL THROUGH TIME.

SWORD, SHIELD, GAUNTLETS, BREASTPLATE, BOOTS AND HELMET.

BUT TOGETHER, THEY MAKE YOU IMPOSSIBLE TO BEAT.

THE VIKINGS ALREADY HAVE THE SWORD AND THE SHIELD.

TRUE - BUT THEY WON'T GET THE BREASTPLATE. IT POWERS THIS SHIP!

AND WE KNOW WHERE THE OTHER THREE ITEMS ARE.

DON'T WORRY, WE'LL GET YOUR SISTER BACK!

TIME TO GO BACK TO THE FUTURE!

BEEP!

THE FUTURE.

FLYING CARS! COOL! DO WE HAVE JETPACKS YET?

SORRY, BUT SAYING **ANYTHING** TO YOU COULD AFFECT YOUR OWN FUTURE.

BUT BASICALLY, YES.

WHY ARE YOU DRESSED LIKE THAT?

T-REXES SCARE PEOPLE. I'M IN DISGUISE.

OH, THAT WORKS. THEY'LL NEVER THINK YOU'RE A **DINOSAUR IN A SUIT.**

LONDON - PRESENT DAY.

HERE YOU GO, GIRLS! THE **EXACT** TIME AND PLACE YOU LEFT!

THANKS, CAPTAIN CLOCK! GOOD LUCK FINDING THE TIME VIKINGS!

HOLD ON - THIS ISN'T RIGHT.

WHY ARE THE PEOPLE DRESSED LIKE **VIKINGS** --

-- AND WHEN DID **THAT** GET HERE?

HELLO, WE'RE DOING A **SCHOOL PROJECT.**

WHEN DID THE VIKINGS WIN?

YOU MEAN WHEN DID KING YORGEN THE FIRST RULE?

THAT WAS AFTER HE BEAT **ALFRED THE PRETENDER** IN **878 CE.**

878 IS WHEN ALFRED 'THE GREAT' **DEFEATED** THE VIKINGS AND MADE PEACE WITH THEM.

HE WASN'T THAT GREAT. I HEARD HE WAS A **RUBBISH** BAKER.

WE CAN'T LET THIS HAPPEN! KING ALFRED IS MY GREAT GRANDFATHER - WELL, TIMES THIRTY.

THIS ISN'T YOUR HOME - DO YOU WANT TO COME WITH US AGAIN AND PUT THINGS RIGHT?

DEFINITELY!

MUM! WE MISSED YOU!

BUT I'VE ONLY BEEN IN THE SHOP FOR **FIVE** MINUTES!

WHERE DID JESSIE GET THAT COSTUME?

WE WERE TAKEN BY **TIME VIKINGS!** AND I JOINED THEIR CREW, BUT THEY THREW ME OUT.

AND THEN WE WENT TO THE FUTURE! AND THEN WE MET A BAKER CALLED ALFRED.

SHOPPING

THAT'S NICE DEAR.

GOODBYE, CAPTAIN CLOCK.

I HOPE I SEE YOU ALL AGAIN ONE DAY.